The
Latitude
of a
Mercy

Other Books by Stefan Lovasik

Persona and Shadow
Absolution

The Latitude of a Mercy

poems

Stefan Lovasik

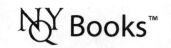

The New York Quarterly Foundation, Inc.
Beacon, New York

NYQ Books™ is an imprint of The New York Quarterly Foundation, Inc.

The New York Quarterly Foundation, Inc.
P. O. Box 470
Beacon, NY 12508

www.nyq.org

First Edition

Set in New Baskerville

Layout and Design by Raymond P. Hammond

Cover Art: "The Latitude of a Mercy," 17.5" x 11.5", acrylic on paper
  by Jean Kondo Weigl, 2021

Author Photo by Elias Vance-Lovasik

Library of Congress Control Number: 2021935094

ISBN: 978-1-63045-086-1

for Cynthia & Elias

&

in memoriam, Lawrence & Rosemary Lovasik

CONTENTS

The
Latitude
of a
Mercy

"Out of the horror there rises a musical ache that is beautiful..."

—James Wright

"Some of them died.
Some of them were not allowed to."

—Bruce Weigl, *Elegy*

Contact

here the beast
still breathes
its burning stone
hearing men alone
fight into death

in a world
that cannot be named
I rise and fall

in the goddamn noise
that splits you in two

The River

Moving up river to Phnom Ke
bones hang from trees,
bodies float in a ring
of yellow and green.
I hear children.
The disemboweled lie
in twisted angles
on the shoreline;
stench opens my throat.
I see children
play with a red ball,
pushing the dead
to make enough space.
I hear them sing.
They smile and wave
as if to welcome me,
as if this beautiful green
death is worth keeping.

Get Ready

When I got to him,
JB was trying to put his tongue back
Through the blown-out flesh
That used to be his cheek.
Legs bent under him
In this patch of boiling dirt
And bent metal,
In this heat of nowhere;
The razor grass shredded
With spider webs of blood
Filling in the spaces between the blades.
As I tried to help, I started to sing
Get Ready by the Temps.
By the end of the first verse,
He rattled in the sun.
He was ready and gone.

As I walked away, I was still singing—

You motherfuckers.

Letter # 1

J. — 7 months here in nowhere—the northwest corner
of South Viet Nam called Lang Vei, about 3 klicks east of
Laos & 9 klicks west of Khe Sanh, Hwy. 9, McNamara line...
nothing good happens here. The suffering & horror in this
beauty is beyond words & the Pathet lao have taken atrocity
to a new level. So, I've gone primal and I'm at peace &
therefore making my case, my argument to the council of
the dead to *belong*, to prove myself worthy. I'll ignore cries &
screams. If we make it out alive tomorrow, I'll probably grill
fish with some of my Chinese Nung & Montagnard buddies.
They're some of the bravest I've seen. Old school: hatchets,
up close & personal, even bow & arrow. The sound of the
arrows fly gives one a disturbing, but yet satisfying, oddly
familiar feeling: an ancestral connection & I have never
felt such fear, yet *fully present & fully alive,* especially during
& after the contact, the engagement...then misery snakes
its way into you deep...then peace & misery on a loop...no
words for this, no sense...so, fuck it...
... today I'll trip off to somewhere in my head, like
Abyssinia, to discuss poetry with Art Rimbaud or imagine
starting a band back in Cleveland. I can go anywhere in this
place of absolute peace, absolute misery. The dead know
the con of the peaceful garden without its opposite. I see it
in their eyes. Last night, St. John of the Cross & St. Teresa of
Avila came to visit. Great talk. They understand.—S.

Hunky Dory at Lang Vei

after the fire-fight that day

after the smoke and screams

were sucked back into the jungle

after the dying

we had some hours of rest at lang vei

bowie on the box

we loved it

he looked like lauren bacall
on the cover

we loved it
for the hours we were given

we sang along
we sang to make it through

to make it through what was
going through our heads

what and who was next

Primal

we are prey
to our oblivion

you or me
in a blast of white

phosphorous & orange
orchids & birds

fall as fire washes
the green & we see

skin burn to grimace
stretch across black

teeth & know flame
will always sing

your fear & mine
vein the leaves

the grass as i press
my hand to the ground

to know your pulse
your moves the way

an animal can sense
rain this fullness

of nowhere pure
moment in pure now

absence & presence
as i cut & pull

feel your life
cover me

from howl to cry

Letter # 2

J.—I will bivouac tonight in a black star tree, above the jungle's crawl, the damp that will rot you. I won't be able to get high enough to get a little light from the moon that is so close & the night sky that seems to be too small to hold the stars— the triple canopy won't allow it.

It will be pitch black, like so many nights. I mean the kind of dark where you can't tell if your eyes are open or closed. Nothing to be seen, only felt & heard & tasted & smelled. In this black & in the sun & heat that swallows you, my fear is that my breathing and heartbeat will give me away, get me dead, no matter how high I go or where I go. There's a name for this that tunnel rats came up with: *black echo*... goddamn right, but the echo stays with you, pounds its way in deep.

In this dark, I'll go to that *first, primordial* savannah, in first moonglow, with no name & naked, just hunger & a sense of awe, ready for the kill with no choices.

I'll be ok if I keep myself open to the visions, the jungle's radiant green that burns behind my eyes. My God, such beauty here, such beauty.—S.

Meditation Near the Waterfall at Dak To

I want to be debriefed
Someone to say something that makes sense
Someone to stroke my hair
The sun to fall
I want the smell of blood & oil
Like the liftships at LZ Brown
& the smell of open wounds & damp rice
Like the whole goddamn beautiful country
To become lavender & bread
I want the dead to get up & weep

I will shrink into a bullet
& explode into somewhere
Far away way down anywhere

& sleep

Letter # 3

J.—this afternoon we lit up another VC encampment, a village really. Men, women, girls & boys that were no more than 11 or 12…it's hard to say how old. My stomach keeps turning.

All armed, firing—some of the younger ones tossing grenades at us, running at us, screaming… some smiling. My stomach is turning. I can't get their faces out of my head. So here I sit with a bottle of cognac that we found & the 4 of us silent. I got up & took a few steps, & my stomach turned, then the other 3 stomachs turned. This is eating a hole in us, & I don't know how much more is left, but I have to swallow it & keep moving. It seems like we pass easily from horror & brutality to contentment, peace, even a glimpse of the eternal now. I know this: too much light or too much dark will drive you to the edge. I need a bit of light. Pray for light.—S.

Primal Baby

Fever and banging drum—
your damp voice wails
in the hollow bamboo.
The black star trees bend,
and again miseries
trumpet your presence.
So, please, take me
primal baby to dance
in this sanctuary,
where blood lingers
before dawn, that moment
before the close of an eye,
before the hopeless
prayer, before the kill.
I need to feel you move
in my hands, how to embrace you.
Inviolate, horrible baby sharpen
my skills, show me your resolve,
your secrets, that I may live.

Letter # 4

J.—found out that I'm 29 days short & a wake up & I can't think about it. Have to stoke the fires of my superstitions, compulsions & obsessions that got me this far: left boot on first, gear & weapons cleaned in a particular order, put on gear & sling weapons in a particular order, check myself & everything 5 times, exactly 5 times, sing 2 secret songs in my head before moving out…it goes on & on. In a way, I don't want to leave. We're the best & I'm good at this. What the fuck am I going to do back in the world? Dedicate myself to kindness & compassion? Be a lifer & wait for another war? Re-up for another tour? I've done & seen enough. I have this sense that I'm spoiling like a piece of meat in the sun. Who knows? At the very least, everything I do will be compensatory in some way, but the plane home will probably go down, so nothing to worry about. In the meantime, we go into the bush tomorrow for about a week. Got my steroid shots & a resupply of my medical gear: codeine, darvon, dexedrine, penicillin, morphine syrettes, bandages, needle & thread. I don't know J., but tonight I'll go to some of those places in my head: walk the Ebert Strasse in snow & then the promenades of Prague in amber glow, then slip into that zone, into Eden. From my garden of beautiful hell, here's to a fluid rebirth.—S.

The Last Mission

year of the rat
month of ears and skulls
twenty-four days short
and in a crawl to save
what is left of me
to kill whatever fills my scope
whatever enters this green
field of death that has torn us open
our screams a chorus of long vowels
that fall in the tall grass

i think i hear you call my name
i think of your last kiss
your warm breath
but i know this is where misery
gave birth to something worse
i want a blessing
to be given over to whatever god

i don't remember the blast of light
but i'm sure you were there
your kiss hard
your breath that covers me

Monkey

please say hello to my monkey
my funny monkey
my smiling monkey
brutal monkey
holy

i am monkey and monkey is me
in me
with me
always my monkey

eyes my monkey
teeth and brain
we are the jungle blood
find impossible places
to hide and dance and seek

during the day we eat
bananas and bushes
at night we tear flesh
and toast it with lemons and tongues

we tell stories
rehearse all the myths
discuss the elements of the psyche
without speaking

we are the place where secrets are buried
we are the language not spoken
that place where the opposites disappear

that moonless jungle within all creatures
forbidden and desired
we are the shadow monkey

lovely monkey
kind cruel perfect

my complete monkey me
our dance about to begin

so please say hello
we've already eaten
and we're just lying here

on our monkey bones

waiting

Confession

Even fifty years after going over the line,
Pulling the trigger and cleaning the knife
Too many times, I can only speak to you
In a voice of sharp sticks and throat of broken glass.
Out of the jungles of confession, it is this simple:
Some things you don't talk about
Until you have become someone else.
Even now, this *other* speaks to you,

And for this, I can't be forgiven.

Absolution

i.

birthed in the red clay
of georgia and carolina
men in green suits
handed me weapons
mosquitoes and snakes
taught me
the predator's compass
to breathe
to find the opening
draw blood
the sway of pines and flight
of crows the trajectory
of the kill
the swamps my altar

ii.

(as a boy I stood
before an altar of white
I sought all things holy
in darkness I questioned the Mysteries
I opened my heart to all sacraments
Introibo ad altare Dei

I will go to the altar of God)

iii.

i crowned myself
with razor wire
walked into the black
waters to drain
my blood
shed my skin
while they whispered
one shot
one shot one kill
kill one one shot
one shot kill

iv.

(I lit candles
I wanted to become a monk
explore the tabernacle
drink the sacramental wine
Domine exaudi orationem meam
Et clamor meus ad te veniat

O Lord hear my prayer
And let my cry come to you)

v.

from over a thousand yards
i was perfect
and they screamed
they handed me medals
trophies
a beret
with the assassin's pin
i made a covenant with darkness
shaved my head
painted my face the colors
of my altar
filled my veins
with the holy pagan waters

vi.

(the tabernacle was empty
holy water clouded with semen
I renounced light
I began to genuflect to chaos
chanted vespers to rage
Ut indulgere digeneris
omnia peccata mea

Deign in your mercy
to pardon me all my sins)

vii.

i slithered into dog day
all souls day
year of the dead
from chantrea to lang vei
they didn't know the force
of the ground coming up
the speed at which blood flows
they didn't know
how their bodies would twist
into cruel angles
the immediacy of nothing

viii.

(I walked into blackness
that warmed me
I wanted to burn
to kill
to kill
Confiteor Deo omnipotenti

I confess to Almighty God)

ix.

they will never know
how their bones and blood
shake me from sleep
they will never know
how i carry them like stones
my black waters heart
that continues to break
and moves me
that boy
    libera nos a malo
    Deliver us from evil
to this absolution I still seek

Returning to the World

for James M. Desmone, Charlie Co.
Air Calvary 1ˢᵗ of the 12th

Returning to the world in seventy-three,
Jim and I walked
The Narraganset beach;
Tried to feel the clams with our feet,
Tried to feel *here*.
Back at the house, friends
Rolled joints in multi-colored papers
And tried to forget the distance,
Our long stare.
We just wanted the clams,
But the smell brought the bloated bodies
In the red paddies
Into sharp focus, and we were *there*.
The bark of orders to execute
The young, small men
At close range,
The bits of skull that shot
Backward onto our lips,
That shot all the way back
To Narragansett
As we fell into the sand—
Prayed for the waves, the tide
To bring us something good.
It never did.
Only the smell remains.

How It Feels

When I go dark,
                a lovely snake unwinds in me—
a second and third eye lid covers my sight,
                so I see through all objects and people
until something dead begins to grow
                and I want everything
to burn,
                to cover myself in fetid oils
because nothing good is here with me.
                Nothing can survive
the decay in my spine
                that flows,
familiar and satisfying
                as anything made of light—
the beautiful tremor in my throat
                ready to give way.
I want to soak in this darkness
                then cover us in my ashes.

Self-Portrait at 23 after ECT

The ash of Lang Vei
On the tip of yr tongue,
The red of Hwy. 9 flows
Where shadows nail
Gallows of jungle as the Fates
Rustle a noose.
You expected the voodoo
To work, the ethereal Queen
To make memory sleep,
But the dark King pulls the pistol
In the dark corners of the green
War you carry, and only gods
Don't remember:
The shaman's blessing didn't take,
Lovely fucking amnesia—
Wait for the *words*,
That other vision of another
World you saw.

A Little Shade

It's sometimes that particular low, gray light of morning
    or a brilliant moon that swallows me, lights
the glare of my history, puts it into that dark wish to erase.
    Those times when I had one eye on those deaths
in the circle of the scope, and one eye on the beautiful green;
    the sway of it, the silent track of birds. That fire of days
and nights I had to love to make it through.

So, yes, I want a little shade like the dark and opiate jungle rain.

Persona

I fashion it with fragments of bone and wire:

An image crafted so well,
So clean,
So foul.

This hard film of skin
I know too well: my tough fool of zeroes,

This life like a language of one vowel.

Day Vision

for Chanté Wolf

Breeze through the window interrupts
The blurred and suffused light of children
Who pour rice into clay bowls as they burn,
The green vines that hold the doors shut
And grow over my faint space of unraveling.
For a moment, like the sigh of a shiver, this frail
Wind comes as if it's a last breath, the smell of flesh
Burned, but it's wood, and I know to wait
Among the broken and bloody lilies,
And let the jungle have its way.

Falling

Years ago, I tried to tell you
That there were ghosts in me,
Beside me,
Attachments gone, I was alien
To our species,
Falling back into the jungle,

Tried to tell you it was ok.
I live in two worlds.

Hand to Hand

I wish I knew less about killing
without a bullet. Where to strike
to make the body crumble and seize
with a finger,
a stick,
a fist,
so your legs won't work
and your eyes bleed.
I can do this in the time
it takes you to draw one more
breath before your last,
and there's no other way to say this.

Personas

for Rob "Tiger" K.

can you recall how we thought
to maintain these masks carefully constructed
to fit every occasion
every nuance

to escape the memory
the fear
to hide and be known
to notice

in the throat of night's doubt
those clear points along the way
along silver threads that hold us
to ground and sky

that we lost ourselves
only to find ourselves
to see what we have always known

the disturbingly authentic naked face

Lesson in the Dharma # 1

the monk from kontum tells me
        to gather my years together
into a circle to say
        thank you then let it go
leave things be

cold wind blasts down through thick
        heat cracks the cisterns
of the lies that burrow into
        my skin as the jungle grows around me
the chorus of noise becomes
        a sermon of gratitude

and i wake like a twisting wire
        knowing that all these years
i've been hearing the same sound
        all dying creatures make

The Prayer

After the war, we started to walk
Through dark rooms to find
A prayer to believe, a breath
Of mercy to blow down
From our black memory,
Our disturbed sky
To draw us up
So we could look down
And find the pieces lost
Among the dead;
To remove the stain of our fury,
To bless the jungle's green
Where blood once washed it into red—
To see the prayer written in the eyes
Of those left behind, to hold them
Until we remember nothing
But light, and die into grace
As the prayer that can never be denied.

Song of the Dead

In the blistered jungle we were born,
Canopies of green, floor of bones.
We found our death, our voice in the song of the dead alone.

And from the mortar rounds we saw our death,
From the bouncing mines we found a cadence to sing our song;
The bodies of the broken, the song of the dead alone.

The compass of reason, our way home lost,
We became an explosion of wounds and heard beyond the rhythm of moans,
The gaze of our death, our voice among the dead alone.

From the impossible jungle we were birthed,
Never to return to the homes we lost, the voices once heard,
Yet the thunder is still the mortar rounds, lightning the cracking of bones:
To find ourselves again, our voice again in the song of the dead alone.

Veterans Day

the day is pressed flat against the monument

near the bridge we walked as boys

near the river where we proved we were men

by swimming its width

where spirits now gather

helping us to piece together how we survived

the jungle's rage and the boys squeezing the triggers

as we stand in the gleam of this hard stone

knowing our memories are exit wounds

thinking tropical in cold wind

remembering the glory we swallowed

to become the blood men

the chasm men

thinking mercy

will hear our buried voices

Lesson in the Dharma #2

The world will be simple,
Empty as air as we flow
Through each other,
Look beyond the weight
Of knowing and illusion
Of happiness, with our slight
Smiles to the darkness
Where we welcome ourselves
And rejoice in the fullness
Of nothing, our silence:
Our first, exquisite delusion.

Shining World

after Bruce Bond

What doesn't kill us
Breaks us into pieces;
Blows out the stray candles
Of our hope as we chatter
Empty as wind.
How obvious we become, lost
In our anger, our tremendous dark
Parade of years to undo the grief,
What grows in us.
Our humanity a question that echoes
Inside; the will to do good, do better
Or a way out. A momentary comfort
Like a child's wish to forget.
But to know it is not always grace or strength,
But a burden we have no choice
But to live inside the echoes,
Inside the chaos. To lie down
In our hurt and loss, feel their beauty;
The way they lift us
To that shining world,
Inside this one,
We will never fully know.

At the End of My Rope

in the rain
in the low red of weeds & mud
an ecstasy spoke to me
so i waited for my second infinity
a radiance to bring a few words

all that had deserted me

it rained & soaked in
as syllables formed
one blood lotus blossomed

in the dead who followed me

whose voice rose
in the threads of my unraveling

so i could speak to you

so i may live among you

Spiritus Contra Spiritum

for J.

We know the brilliant palette of our inscapes that create new elements. The crystal and sorrow of bridges that cover the planets of our Shadows that propel us. When mixed with the Castalian waters, the Beast swelled. Our last holy drink when we dined precisely at the time the tension of opposites were arcing and folded into ten languages.

We committed to simple steps, a periodic table to forge a new music to carry our souls' face. Yet our clear eyes are second guessed—we continue to autopsy the years of dark corridors and find ways to defy and find the tablatures of those old tears; the alchemy of precise words and cuts, the concoction of diamonds and loss.

Nonetheless, a new music swallowed, a sober rising in this brilliance: Spiritus contra Spiritum the refrain, yet vigilance carries a noose.

Sacrifice and crucifixion are still on the table. Don't be fooled— we are so far from who we think we are.

Rush

weight grace

       gravity of blessings

to still breathe yet

       something violent and shining

between the shoulders

       draw tendons out

blasts holy my darkened wounds

that beat like wings

       that beat to the radiant green

no reason to leave

       these safe boundaries

tedious comforts

       half-alive but

go back where we walked

       through that rush of beautiful terror

feel that tiger moon

       our lovely jungle

light up our blood

Reincarnate

for Dr. Vivian Y.

In our eyes we saw a river,
Like the river near Ca Lu
Where I saw her rise
Above the dust and tears.
My eyes protector,
Hers a grace, that lifted us
Above the jungle,
Above the disturbing world,
And we danced
In my suit of blood,
Her grief-jeweled áo dài*
As our river filled us—
Let our bodies open
Into the flow of constant
Waters that break into this day.

---

*pronounced "owzeye": a traditional, tunic-like dress worn over
pants in Viet Nam

The Disassociation of 50 Winters

In the empty field
my dull head hums
the old explosions
and dark hymns.

You hold out your hand
as I reach through
the black shake of jungle,
to the valley where curses

flow in the luminous green,
then feel your hand
as we walk through
the deep December snow.

The Noble Science of Trauma

for CVL

I shower in the canopied jungle with wires of light
and rain; dry with strings of ears and scalps,
I step into your body, a mirror. My faces
sweat liquid only the dead can give up,
yet the mirror rips into a thousand scars,
the age of my eyes. I lie down in thin night,

in white phosphorous, until you remind me
that the light is from stars, and the moon, over St. Paul,
breaking. I want to tell how I try
to forgive *this boy*, but here beside you
this old man pulls the trigger as I hold
and cannot hold your beautiful hand. Turn
toward a burning face in the night's window, blossom.

Shut Down

Understanding less,
nights are refuge
to hear uncertain distances
like decades past,
yet another piece
of the puzzle
falls apart and you
can't see
what visions
used to be,
knowing it was there,
at some point
important, vital;
at some point
wanting to do it right
or take it all back.

I don't know,
these nights do not last.
So, now, I'll choose
my sounds and visions—

don't tempt me to seek or be reasonable;

don't ask me anything.
Everything now ends at my fingertips.

Projections

"People need a few things: air, water, food, shelter and someone or something to blame."
—Rabbi A. Twerski, M.D.

Again, we talk—the typical routine

Of our complexes, the pantomime

Of dissonant autobiographies

Exposing the low burn of loss and shame;

What we now blame and paint the mirrors

Of our delusions to reflect only the perfect

Ghosts of what we think we are, our poor

Diamonds of expectations and perceptions

Of being complete over this expanse of time;

Safe in the illuminations of our amnesia

The comfort of our disdain, our fever of difference.

Blind in the expected labyrinths of self,

Refusing to enter these nights of the soul

And now find in our rage we are screaming

The looping satryicon of our lies to step

Through these mirrors and become

What we have always despised—

Our diseased projections, our paralysis
In these damaged arcs to become

Someone, something.

Hard for Jesus

Fresh, bloody and crazy from the jungle, I couldn't walk down any street without being confronted by the Jesus-freak jagoffs: "Have you accepted Jesus Christ as your Lord and Savior?" I would spit out, "I've accepted Jesus H. Christ as a zen buddhist jew!" or "I've accepted Jesus from Tijuana as my fuck-buddy!", and they would scream, "Jesus is Coming!"

I would snap back, "See, I didn't know he was still fucking! That prick!"

In all their self-righteous bullshit, godly calm and misguided missionary work, their eyes turned red. I could smell their hate, but one day in '73 I met Jesus on the corner of Center and Liberty. When I asked her name, she said, "I AM (long pause) the Christ." She was beautiful. A glow of gold and violet filled the street. Her deep-set green eyes pierced me. Turned out, she was a waitress at an Italian joint down the street...my kind of God.

We wound up at her garage apartment that smelled like burnt toast and tore into each other, our tongues explored each other. A preview of heaven, I thought?

As we made love, Christ said she saw COLORS and kept blessing me. I was in heaven, again and again and again.

It was glorious, I saw the angels with my hard-on for Jesus and screamed, "Oh, my God! Oh, Christ! Oh, my God!" and she was yelling, "Yes, my son! Yes, my son! Oh, Yes my son!"

...and I was transported, changed and I *knew* God was *woman*.

A Toast to my Fellow Citizens

I'm not here again,
At the lovely table
As we raise our glasses.
My body of camouflage

In the heavy bamboo chair
Beside you, the green vines
That pull me into the heat,
The screams at LZ Blue.

I hear your words fall inside
The wire, the thump of mortars
And my black echo of breath
As I rise in a needle of light
From the damp jungle floor.

So please, extend your hands
That I may find you again,
The moment our glasses touch.

The Foundry, 1960

for Bruce Weigl,
in memory of Albert Weigl 1923–2018
& Lawrence Lovasik 1920–1995

We run through slag and ash,
play soldier, good at dying,
then walk in the stiff green water
near funnels of smoke where whistles
ring for home, and another stack of tens and quarters.
We watch the burial of fish and almost see
the virus in the river that bent our friend's legs
as barges crush toward the foundry
where our fathers were burning;
thought of how it would be to stand
with them in the heat, their skin
probably crackling in the silver suits;
wondered how it would be to walk
by the odd green water, to laugh
our way to the bar and feel good
about the extra sawbuck we had
to throw back a couple of shots and beers;
buy the biggest turkey for Thanksgiving—
and we still wonder what it would be like
to have that life they showed us.
Even through the furious, green war
they stood with us in the heat
as they do now in cold wind,
to bend down and kiss us,
to let us know how to live.

King of Dirt

In 1960 at St. Al's, the Pittsburgh sun suspended
by soot and ash, the Allegheny catfish sick with polio,
it was catholic recess, the holy recess.
A holy dog of a boy argued with me
about the vital importance of the accordion
in a band. I responded, "No, I think the drums
are more important." Some pushing began,
a few punches thrown, and I thought,

this is how people think, I'm fuckin' doomed.
So, I ran up stood on the playground's
mound of dirt and sure enough this boy,
big as a '56 Olds, charged at me,
wanted to knock me off, knock me down.
His small colorless eyes, his large forehead led the way,
and I realized *this is hate on its way,* and suddenly
I didn't care. I was a martyr. King of Dirt, buddy.
All the dead languages standing on the mound.
Bothered by no history, I was original, different.
I was *Rex Imperfundies.* *

What got to me was the thought of his *ideas,*
and all of those that came before him.
The same stupidity, and same eyes, the hatred,
The long heavy-handed idiocy
and shadow of the centuries.

---

*King of Dirt

The Last Catechism

Pin those lips, son.
Listen the words of Jesus.
I'll try to explain and kill you,
If that is what it takes.

But, Father, I see dark in you,
A spine of shadows; the bloody
Crucifix under your chin, the dead bird
in your desk that you told me was Lazarus.
It's been there a year.

Please, Father, I hear you.
Jesus is here, outside, holding His nose,
Looking at His watch. He looks old
And gray and sad.
And yes, Father, I feel you;

Your hand on my small cock,
Your stale air of sweat and shame
Trying to explain
The methods of being ridiculous, holy,
Pure, then saved by your hand,
By that terrible, confused God.

O, lurid Dominie!
Your savior ignored my prayer,
My salvation.

Father

He wore fourth hand-me-downs
as a kid. Fashioned cardboard
soles for one pair of shoes
that he blackened with polish
to hide the holes.

But he walked and learned
a stilted english that felt like gristle
on his tongue, and he walked toward
the idea of having real shoes,
having a clean tongue,

a clear sentence. Yet he walked
and when the sentence came,
the tongue in place and smooth,
he bought blue shoes, red, yellow,
white, suede, two-tones—

hundreds of shoes that replaced
the dirt floors, five brothers
to a bed, the odor of urine
and dumplings, old chicken.

So, he walked in the purple shoes,
tan, green, true black.
He walked against all of it:
the incessant vapid chatter of pretense,
the poverty, the piety.

This savagely intelligent clown
making his way, playing it like jazz.
His walk, like a thin buddha, almost complete

as he embraced me, lifted me with my boots.

First Sight

for my son

When I first saw you, I knew you.
Your face as familiar as mine
As if I had seen it decades before.
Your small hands that covered me,
That opened my secrets and brutalities,
So that I could get up from the table
To find my way, and you could find yours.

I will know you, this love,
And we will always meet
In that light that lingers above
The waters of our birth.

Mother's Day

First woman—lonely, old
Child who bites at air,
Your dollhouse lights
The roses in your hand
For my birth tied pretty
In a bow, and the years
An object
For display.

I called for you,
Your ornamental,
Medaled son,
Once, when you were there,
Then never again, that love.

The Alchemy of Age

for Dan Ryan

Late in this go-a-round, secrets harden
into something like small coins to count,
lay out on a table, or put into pockets
that have appeared with the alchemy of age—

that weight that slips in deep,
widens the hole inside
that swallows you again
and the coins drop:

your brothers stringing ears and scalps
together in the low sun of the jungle
as a pig turned on a spit,
or the rape you didn't stop, the child
you let die, and you realize
it was the same little girl you saw near Ca Lu
who placed a severed foot beside
the stump of a dead boy's arm
as if to complete it, to make it better,
then smiled at you and skipped
toward the stink of the river, all the way
back into your fifty-year grief—
her beautiful face, her small fingers
pressed to your lips.

Some things are better left buried deep.

The Impossibility of Reason
for Butch

It was the green, the maple leaves
Turning their light side toward
The broken spaces between our words,

The red-tailed hawks that break
And pivot into our stories—
Our conversation of grace,

The impossibility of reason,
How we got here from the red
Mist of Ca Lu and Khe Sanh—

The distractions of years
And gravity that numbs us
As to why we sit here

As old men yet boys
Rehearsing a method to live
In this world and wonder

Why the truth still sounds like a lie.

Oberlin, Ohio
June, 2019

Response to "Why Don't You Stop Writing about the War and Forget about It"

*Đu ma**

A child's cry in the burning hooch.
The rot.
The beautiful Hmong, the Vietnamese,
Their blood, their thousand-year grief,
Their tongues in small pots.
The trigger you never squeezed.
The telegram never received.

All that has been forgotten,
And will be forgotten again.
The violence in you denied,
The brutality just under your sleep.

The loss,
The lost.

*Bui doi, bui doi***

---

*motherfucker
**children of the dust

A Momentary Dance with the Eternal Now

spirit

    as crescent stone
drape of water

    river of blossom
palm of sun
    empty

in flow
    one center
in light
    absent perfection

an immensity
    behind my eyes
gone
    to what god

Elegy for Nguyễn Quảng Đào

Tchepone, Laos 1971

February's tired hand
closes around the lilies.
The night air like silk,
streams of still water
hold the rotation of stars
in your eyes. You are
feather, black wing
above the wounds,
above the stripped brown
mountains and trees
that wave their bloody
limbs in the constant
light of bodies
ascending, the requiem
of the night bird's
rising call.

Old Soldier

Here you are, Mr. Shiny Head,
Wearing your hair bald
Because there's no longer a choice,
Old soldier, here in your seventy years.
Your wife, her constant love,
In the other room reading,
A way to get some distance
From that hole inside of you:
What you did, what you saw
And couldn't bear to tell
When the secrets couldn't hold,
Even when it all came back—
That fear of losing her, being alone
Like you are now trying to write
Something down to draw people
Into those years, yet you know
They will never understand
What they told you:
You are not here, kill it all, kill it all.

The Latitude of a Mercy

for my wife

For that time lived among strange flowers,
Baptized in red, warm water
Where no god would go,
Paid witness too soon,
I thought in grids and lines—
The coordinates of survival,
But saw in fractured light spirits gathered
At points in the radiant green
That spoke to me,
Who held me
To the latitude of a mercy,
A way to get home
To that summer when we kissed hard
Listening to Etta James and Marvin Gaye,
Bells and whistles from the Allegheny
Telling me there could be other nights
Time would draw out forever;
Not this life dropped and broken,
Beyond hope and those nights,
But a walk with those spirits
To now—along one, impossible line

Acknowledgments

Grateful acknowledgment is made to the editors of the following publications in which many of these poems first appeared: *The American Literary Review, Blackbird, BuffaloX, Consequence, First Literary Review, Folio, Frameworks, Gravel, Hanley Arts & Letters, Hiram Poetry Review, Main Street Rag, The McNeese Review, Meat for Tea: The Valley Review, The New York Quarterly, Offcourse Literary Journal, Pedestal Magazine* and *Rust & Moth Literary*.

Additionally, versions of: "The River," "Get Ready," "Hunky Dory at Lang Vei," "The Last Mission," "Monkey," "Confession," "Absolution," "Returning to the World," "How It Feels," "The Prayer," "Persona," "Veterans Day," "Projections," "Hard for Jesus," "Hand to Hand," and "King of Dirt" also appeared in *Absolution* (Main Street Rag Publishing Co., 2018).

"The Foundry, 1960" appears in the anthology *Without a Doubt: poems illuminating faith* (NYQ Books, 2021).

The author would also like to extend his enduring gratitude to the following people for their special assistance, friendship and support: John Amen, Tom Anderson, Jan Beatty, Bryan Bodrog, Bruce Bond, Stacey Chambers, James M. Desmone, Raymond Hammond, Dr. K., Jered Mundt, Tim Nolan, Thia Powers, Dan Ryan, Dr. John P. Shallcross, Daniel Starks, Brian Turner, Mai Der Vang, Bruce Weigl, Jean Kondo Weigl, Chanté Wolf, and the Warrior Writers/Twin Cities community.

About the Author

photo by Elias Vance-Lovasik

Stefan Lovasik served with U.S. Army Special Forces during the American war in Viet Nam. His poetry has appeared in the *American Literary Review, Consequence, Folio, Hiram Poetry Review, New York Quarterly,* and *Pedestal* among others. He has published two collections: *Persona and Shadow* (FlutterPress, 2015) and *Absolution* (Main Street Rag Publishing Co., 2018).

CPSIA information can be obtained
at www.ICGtesting.com
Printed in the USA
FSHW010533070421
80184FS

9 781630 450861